# Things I

# Wish

# I Knew...

♥

*Never compromise your authenticity for the comfort of others....*

*-k.m. brady*

♥

This book is dedicated to anyone that is walking, stumbling or crawling through life trying to figure out where they belong. This is a collection of poems I've written over the course of my life during different stages of things that were happy, bad, or even devastating. Writing is how I process them.

To my inspirations for all I do in this world, my daughters, being your mother has been the greatest gift that God has bestowed upon me other than breathing. You make me whole and give me the strength and courage to be unapologetically myself in all I do. Loving you and watching you grow into women has been my honor and absolute joy. No measure of time is enough with either of you.

To the authors that continuously inspire me to be daring and a better writer, I thank you humbly. Being an independent author is never easy, but with an army of others like you in your corner, it becomes bearable. So, thank you Leah Maye, C.J. Pearson, Ariel Archer, April D. Berry, Golden Angel, Willow Winters, Brittanee Nicole and Angela Montoya. You all inspire me to be a better writer daily. To Dawn Hosmer, you were a light and inspiration to us all, rest in peace and I hope you have found a comfy spot to read and write up there.

Lastly, to all the victims of domestic violence and intimate partner violence, I see you and I am with you. I will fight until my last breath to do what I can to bring awareness and help as many of you as I can.

♥

Why does love hurt?

Why does it feel like burning coals?

Why does it leave you longing for more?

Yearning.

Why do you dislike the way you feel when you hurt?

Why do you drown your sorrows in a bottle to numb it all?

Why do you want to curl up in a ball and cry all day?

Pain.

Because it was love.

Love is messy and unpredictable.

It is painful and beautiful.

Magical and sinful.

It is stumbling through the darkness looking for the light blind.

That is love.

And without it, the world is less colorful.

Less meaningful.

Less beautiful.

♥

Less magical.

Less cheerful.

Less than.

♥

Why does life have to be so difficult?

Everyone expects so much of you.

Hold it together.

Be strong.

Be resilient.

Be brave.

Be bold.

Maybe I just want to curl up with a book, read and tune the world out.

Life, have you ever thought about that?

I've tried holding it together, look where it got us.

I've been strong and it left me alone and crying.

I've been resilient and it just left...me.

I've always been brave, never backed down.

Fat luck that has given me.

Bold, I came out of the womb dripping in boldness.

Life, how about you just back off a bit and let me drink my tea, read my book and I'll be all the

♥

things you want me to be tomorrow?

Deal?

♥

I sit here, questioning everything and everyone.

Why now?

Why at this stage in my life do I question things?

Am I having a midlife crisis?

Am I having a momentary lapse in judgment?

Am I just lonely and my mind has time to wander?

Who knows.

But what I do know is, I am questioning things I never did before.

Looks people give.

Words they say and how they say them.

Flicks of hair by "friends" in conversations.

Social media posts that seem one sided.

Social media posts that are blatant calls for attention.

The actual fakeness in people that I used to look at as genuine and authentic.

Now their words burn my ears and taste like poison.

Betrayal.

♥

Deceit.

Lies.

Games.

Hatred.

Jealousy.

Those same "friends" that put on a show for social media
boasting motivational quotes, yet hate

themselves in the mirror and talk poorly about those they
love.
How do we get so blinded by these kind of people?

How do they infect us with their venom and then devour our
souls?

Only to move on to their next victim so intently without a
second thought.

These are the people that come to you and want to gossip and
talk about others.

It's all fun, until you walk away and they begin to talk about
you.

That knife slid in really easy as you turned around for them,
yet you still remained loyal.

Fool.

♥

## *The Colors*

Purple...

It's so vibrant and direct.

It screams at me, look at me!

And then in that moment when I can't stop staring at all its

hatred, it has the decency to change.

Blue....

Now, you are this less bold, yet still aggressive reminder.

This still forceful color shoved in front of me to stare at.

And then, once I am settled in with it, you change yet again.

Yellow...

Muted in yellow and green and almost faded away.

I find comfort in the disappearance and solace in the fact that

it is not shoved in my face anymore.

But, it is still there.

It is still a color on me that is not supposed to be there.

Why must you continue to do this?

Why must you change colors?

Why must this happen?

♥

Why must it be so transcendent in its pattern of change?

Why must it be so consistent?

Why not pink?

Why not start with another color?

Why purple?

Why so aggressive and in your face?

Why so intent?

Why choose the most vibrant color?

Almost as if it's a bat signal for all to see.

This peacock, this purple.

♥

I see the roundness beginning

I see the strength forming

I see the protective nature growing

I see the beauty in you that you never saw amplified

I watch you endure pain

I watch you endure exhaustion

I watch you feel love

I watch you see love

I feel overwhelmed

I feel lucky

I feel love

I feel protective

I feel scared

Will I be there for every step, every breath?

Will I leave and never return?

Will you let me in again?

I want so much to be in.

I want so much to be there

I have no control

I cling to the bond we have

♥

The one that began when you looked into my eyes

So lovingly, so innocent

It was just us

That will never go away

No matter who comes or goes

That bond will always be there

So, you go, protect and love

And I'll be here when you are ready

Loving and waiting, patiently for that same look

That same smile and that same love we shared

That beautiful night together

Just us

The wind blows through my hair and

I feel the sun shining on

my face

I exhale deeply and intently

I wiggle my toes in the grass

I feel it's cool moisture flow through my body

I begin to pull up pieces and hold them in my hand

I look at them and think about you

I think about all of our plans for our life together

I chuckle to myself and smile

A single tear runs down my cheek and into my palm caressing

the grass with it's hydration

I look up and think about you

Your warm smile

Your strong arms

Your silent way about you

More tears are flowing into my palm

I look down and notice the grass floating in my tears

I chuckle again

♥

I floated through our love like that grass floated through my
tears

I floated through life waiting, wanting...you

Then, I had you

And then...you were gone

I closed my hand up tight, wiped away my tears

Let the cool breeze fill me up again and the sun dry my tears
away

Opened my hand back up and the tears were gone now, only
grass remained

I closed my eyes and threw my head back into the sunlight
and wished this pain away

And then,

I let the grass soaked tears go into the breeze

Along with you

♥

♥

Oh if I could just stop the pain

I would bottle it up and give it to you

I would give you the ache in my stomach when the phone

rings

I would give you the tears that I cry when I lay down at night,

you not by my side

I would give you the future I mourn

I would give you the emptiness inside I feel when I think of a

day without you

I would give you the fear of seeing you with someone else

I would give you the terror of hearing you never loved me

I would give you the exhaustion from oversleeping

I would give you the extra weight from the chocolate I've

devoured in your absence

I would give you the therapy bills I am enduring from you

shattering my world

I would give you the hurt you deserve like I am feeling

But...

I love you

♥

And, I would rather be in agony than see one second of you hurting

So, I endure the hurt and you move on

Not knowing my pain

As it should be

♥

I don't like
what I see
when I look
back at me
I don't like
what I feel

when you look at me

I don't like what I do when you come around

I don't like who I am with you

I hate myself when I am with you

I hate you for making me someone I am not

I hate you for letting me be this way

I hate myself for letting you

♥

Jumbled

Broken

Weary

Lost, Mistaken and displaced

Signals are firing in the wrong directions or some, not at all

Left is right and right is left

The smiling cat in the corner is begging me to join him

And the yellow shapes are asking me to hop in

Your face is distorted

Who are you?

Why are you not telling me?

I hear my thoughts but I don't hear them coming out

Where are they going?

Who stole them?

Get these little thought stealers out of me

I need my intelligence back

I need my stability back

I need me....Go away cat

♥

I pick up the phone to call you

But you don't answer

I drive by your house

But you are not there

I call your work

But you no longer work there

Where are you?

Why have you gone?

When will you be back?

I wait and wait and nothing

♥

I thought of you today

But that is no different than any other day

I thought of how it felt to hold your hand in mine

Of how it felt to look into your eyes

I remembered the way my stomach would flip when you

would look at me and bite your lip

I touch my lip,

Missing your kiss on mine

I close my eyes and there you are

Safe, right where I left you

In my memories

I see you walking towards me smiling

I feel warm and safe

I begin to move towards you

Faster now

But you seem so far away

Your face is becoming faded and dark

Your smile is no longer as bright and warm

Your arms that were once extended, welcoming me in

Are now gone

♥

I run faster

But you fade more

I reach out and touch the gray image that is left of what was

you

Once again, you are out of my reach

♥

Separation is preparation

But, what if I don't want that?

I don't want to separate, to prepare

I want to feel you still

I want to stay with you

I want you in my life, for my life

Why do you want to leave?

Leaving is a cowards way out

Stay

Fight for us

Step up

I want to scream it from the rooftops

I want to bust into your work and make you hear me

But...you want to go

Why should I fight for you to stay?

If I am not worth the fight for you,

Why should I fight for you?

I love you

I hate you

I am so conflicted

♥

Just call me

I just want to hear your voice

I want to feel your arms around me

One last time

Your kiss on my lips again

Your breath on my neck

And your voice, that deep beautiful voice again

But, I will go.

Separate

Prepare

Move on

Leave

♥

I heard our song today

It took me back to that moment

To that day

I remember us in the car the day you picked it

So happy and carefree

Planning our future

Planning our love

We sat in my car

Looking into each others eyes

Hand in hand

While you sang to me our song

I looked at you

That was the day I knew I loved you

I knew that I wanted you and only you

Watching you be so cheesy singing to me and smiling

I fell hard

Very, hard

But....

You let me fall, alone

You picked a song about doing anything for me

♥

Yet you left me like the wind blowing past

You sang a song about giving your heart to me forever

And then ripped it away with no warning and no explanation

I used to love that song

Before it was our song

Then it was ours and it took on a different meaning

Now, when I hear it

It only brings me back to that moment

When you promised me the world and gave me a morsel

♥

I try and wash the filth away

The filth that flows over me after what you did

What you put me through

The embarrassment

The anger

You made me feel dirty

Unclean

Unwashed

Unwanted

Unloved

Filthy

I scrub and scrub

But I never feel free of the filth you instilled

I will forever be a dirty girl

♥

## *You*

My feet won't move

My heart is frozen

My head is jumbled

My hands are numb

I can't leave

I can't move

I can't breathe

I'm stagnant

Barely alive

A shell of my former self

I can cry

I can cry hard

So I do

So much so, that it drowns me

In a sea of my own salty sadness

Still paralyzed

Still unable to leave

Still waiting for.......You

♥

## Curves

Oh how you loved to grab ahold

Hang on and squeeze what would fit in your hands

Admire what wouldn't

I would watch your eyes light up as you would grab and caress

me

My body was your playground

And I was more than willing to have it open anytime for you

Your fingers danced across me like cursive writing

Your lips softly moved around me devouring every inch of me

for your pleasure and mine

Your hands held me so tight I felt like we became one

Our bodies moved so melodically together like our own

personal love song

My curves arched for you as you ran your fingers across them

Savoring every glance and touch

I watch as you lick your lips and then your fingers

Intrigued, I can't stop starring

My body is yours

♥

Do with it as you please

I begin to relax and stare into you

You look up at me

Slowly move towards me, kissing every inch you can find on

your way

Your kiss is sweet and salty

I feel euphoric and exhilarated

You look me in the eyes and our souls become one

And then we connect

It is seamless and powerful

It is strong and slow

You move my hair slowly caressing my face and place a soft

kiss on my forehead

You whisper into my ear, "you are the love of my life"

Our connection becomes more enchanted and intense

Those words, that motion

I could devour that for the rest of my life

You look into my eyes and kiss me softly

Caress my body and then yours shakes and we become one for

one last time

♥

This beautiful moment forever frozen

Forever stained in my mind

Forever ingrained in my heart

Forever encompassed by my body

♥

Don't just sit there looking the way you do

At me the way you do

Smelling the way you do

Smiling at me like you do

Saying what you are saying

Only to leave me

Broken

Watching you fade away

Longing for the scent you left behind

♥

I didn't think of you today

Well, not all day

So that's progress

I didn't cry

Or throw things

THIS time

I smiled

I laughed

I remembered the good

The minimal good

It was so minute that I blinked and it was over

Now I am back to throwing things...

♥

Dawn has come and I open my eyes

The sunlight dances across my room

Putting on the most glorious show

Almost strutting its beauty

I smile and stretch

Searching for the will to move.

And then...

It washes over me

You are gone.

My brief but beautiful moment of serenity is shattered

♥

## *Hurt*

There will be stuff you can't overcome.

That changes you so much that you forget who you used to be.

That hurt, that pain is relevant and you should feel it.

Just don't let it consume you and contain you.

Yes, it will change you, and that's ok.

Let it change you for the better.

Let it mold your decisions about what you won't accept in your life any longer.

Use the hurt to grow and better yourself,

That is how you regain your power.

♥

## *Revel*

Sit back and reflect on what you have in your life.

Sit back and revel in all that you've overcome to this point.

Remember everything that was meant to destroy you,

Yet all it did was make you stronger and more capable.

That right there is something to revel in because it didn't work.

Spread your wings

peacock and be that amazing person you are

That you've been holding back showing the world.

We want to see you!

We want to know you!

We want to be around you!

We want to learn from you!

Be boisterous,

bold and steadfast in your pursuit of happiness.

It looks amazing on you!

♥

# *Past*

A lot of my past, I kept hidden and locked away in a box for no one to know.

Only a select few, and I mean, select and few, know everything.

Every raw detail, every morsel.

Even my book doesn't cover every single facet of my story, but it's a start.

It's how I began to unlock the box

And share the most painful things I had hidden away for no one to know.

Why?

Because the little things I would sneak out to some would have them running away.

It seemed easier and more comfortable for me to just lay it all out there

And hopefully, just maybe it would help someone else in the process.

There are reasons why I am the way I am, and it's rooted in what has happened to me.

So, to truly even remotely understand me, you've gotta read my book.

♥

I joke and say,

"The next guy that wants to date me has to read it and if he still wants to date me after, I will go out with him."

But it's not a joke, it's how I feel.

If a man can handle all I've survived and still want to be in my life, then that is worth exploring.

So, I never wrote my story for the pity or sadness of others,

I've already had my pity parties and they were more glorious

And came with more wine than anyone else could throw at me.

I wrote my story, my most raw and painful truths to help others

That have also had these unspeakable things occur to them.

To show them that **WE ARE NOT OUR TRAUMA!**

Read that again!

We are so much more than that.

♥

## *Broken*

Hug my broken pieces back together, huh?

Will he realize that they are dripping in pain others inflicted?

Will he realize that the insecurities I bare are from painful memories?

Will he hear my story and run as fast as he can?

Will he see the outside and not care to learn the inside?

Will he even care for my happiness at all?

Will he hit me like others before him?

These broken pieces are sharp and staggered.

I hope he's ready with his armor and chisel to break through them.

That's gonna have to be a powerful hug....

♥

## *Apologies*

So many times, people hurt us and simply toss out that word, "sorry" like it's a sneeze.

But, it's not that simple.

Sorry is not a simple word.

Sorry is actually a very complex word.

It's a word that requires ACTION!

It's a word that requires listening.

It's a word that requires accountability.

It's a word that requires change.

It's a word that requires strength.

It's a word that requires inner reflection.

You see, so many throw it out to stifle us and pacify or minimize our feelings and we let them.

There is no alteration to what they've done to merit the use of "sorry" so it will happen again.

There is no inner reflection on why they are doing the said act they need to say "sorry" for, so

again, it will continue.

♥

If the person saying this word doesn't listen to how they've made YOU feel and YOUR need for

THEIR sorry, it will not change.

If this person is a weak person that cares only about themselves, their "sorry" is meaningless

and more about them than you.

Sorry, is more than a word.

Stop throwing it around and expecting others to just accept it because you've said it, unless you

intend to actually mean it.

♥

## *Stones*

Stones are so easy to throw, so others toss them like a cool breeze.

They hit you hard though and diminish pieces of your psyche with each hit.

Some aren't as painful as others.

Some are gut wrenching, soul crushing holes ripping you apart.

While others are merely just little specks picking at you like a scab.

But...

What if instead of letting those stones destroy us, we let them be those very things that build us.

Those stones represent others' hatred and jealousy, not who we actually are.

They only hurt if we let them.

Next time a stone is thrown, catch it!

Place it next to you.

Embrace its ignorance and use that very stone to build your castle to keep these people out.

♥

Build your castle...

catch your stones,

and be your amazing self,

blemishes and all.

♥

## *Not Broken, Just Bent*

I have endured a lot of trauma, yes.

Did I deserve an iota of it? No

Did it make me stronger? Yes

Did it make me bitter? At times, it did.

Did it make me afraid? Yes, and still does.

Do I still get triggered? Yes, sadly, I do.

Does any of this make me less strong or less of a survivor or

less worthy than anyone else, NO!

Yes, I've been hurt in ways that are despicable.

Yes, I've been beaten down and ashamed.

Yes, there are so many things I wish never happened to me, but they did.

I could cower in a corner and cry about them, having a pity

party of one, or I could face them

and heal, grow and move on.

I choose to heal.

I choose to grow.

♥

I choose to move on.

Strength comes from within when we think we can't muster it

up, it is something that shows up

to help us push through the pain of circumstances and
situations.

Strength comes from facing things that we deem

painful and walking away better than you were

before you faced them.

I am strong.

I am bent, not broken.

♥

## *Savior*

Be your own hero!

Don't wait for someone to come running in and pick you up

and fix everything for you.

Sit with your problems and work through them.

If you're in a relationship that's unsafe, make a plan to leave.

♥

## *Spark*

Do more of what sets your soul on fire!

Do more of what makes YOU HAPPY!

Do more of what makes you smile!

Do more of what you want!

Oftentimes we put our own needs

second or even third or fourth

To others' needs in our life while

our desires take a back seat.

Push those to the front seat and let them drive.

Let those desires, wants and dreams guide you.

You will be much happier that way.

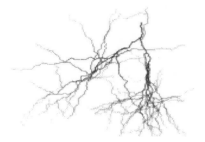

♥

## *Grief*

Grief has no timeline, no rules or regulations.

Everyone grieves differently and sometimes,

They just need someone to listen and hold their hand.

So, I say again, grief has no timeline, rules or regulations.

Just be there, even if you don't understand, or the loss isn't yours.

Just. Be. There.

♥

# *Life*

Life is full of precious gifts

Laughter, Love and Happiness

If we are lucky enough to say we have these things

everyday or want them;

then shower the

world with:

Smiles...Joy...Peace...

and Respect

Then you will receive the same precious gifts in return

and then you will know true

Laughter....Love...and Happiness.

Be kind to one another, it costs NOTHING!

♥

## *Change*

A change is gonna come, it always does....

Sometimes, people say things to you that hurt

Sometimes, people say things that heal

Sometimes, people say things you never expected to hear

Sometimes, you just let go,

move forward and leave things in the past

Apologies that never come are given power if you let it.

Hurt, that cuts you has power if you let it

Chose to move forward

And love those people exactly as they are

Everyone doesn't love the same or speak the same,

But if love is behind it, fault can't be found with it

Just learn to let go

Some people aren't meant for your future

♥

# *Penguin*

I sit back and watch the movie of our love

Of the sweet kisses and long hugs

The beautiful melodic moments where we became one

Those magical explosions between two lovers

Forever you promised

Never did I expect any less

You were my forever, my penguin

My lifelong mate

Just waiting to drop my pebble at your feet

Just waiting for your pebble to come to mine

You must've forgotten what the rules of forever were

Or the meaning of forever

I can't remind you, my sweet penguin

So, instead, I just wait for my pebble.

♥

Change your focus & mindset

Don't live to impress others

Live to progress your life

Live to progress your dreams

Live to progress your goals

Live to progress your happiness

Live to progress your life

Change your focus and mindset and watch everything else

fall into place.

♥

Not my Job

Put on a show for you

Believe your time is more valuable than mine

Allow the scale to define me

My Job:

Use my voice to speak up for what I believe

Work for what I have

Practice self care

Take my medications because my mental health is key

Celebrate my wins and losses

Look for the magic in every day

Love the reflection that looks back at me

Dance like no one's watching, even if they are

Cut ties with anyone that makes me feel less than

Don't care about the opinions of others

♥

## *Walking Away*

Sometimes, walking away from someone

is more about you and less about them.

It's more about your own mental health.

More about your own personal growth.

More about not losing your own identity.

More about not compromising

who you are or your own personal morals for someone else's.

Or maybe that person became everything

you thought they never would.

It's ok to take a step back and assess a relationship

and see if it still "fits" your life.

We try on clothes for the perfect fit.

We try out new hairstyles.

New perfumes.

All of these are trials.

Relationships are trials.

♥

When someone's not meeting your expectations anymore,

no longer bringing you joy, offering

anything to the relationship or hurting you,
their trial offer is over.

There is a reason why we get 90 days to try out at a job,

30-45 days to try out a product.

Don't force any relationship that doesn't fit you!

♥

I

AM

A

PRIORITY

PERIOD

♥

## *Strength*

You hold the key to your inner strength

Breathe, and push through the obstacles in your way trying to break you.

Call a friend & talk out your thoughts, feelings and emotions so you can understand them better.

Begin to solve the issue and you will be able to feel

Relief from the stress of it and the weight it has carried.

Sometimes, you will find that staying silent has more power

Then expressing your feelings in anger to someone that cannot hear them.

Surround yourself with those that listen to hear and not respond.

That is when your strength, love and happiness will flourish.

Never give up, and never give in.

There is always a way.

You may have to turn the problem upside down and look at it a different way

But the answer is there.

It always was

♥

## *Self Care*

Always practice self care.

Maybe it's meditation or yoga.

Running or boxing.

There is a reason that the airline tells you to put on your oxygen mask first

And then someone else's.

YOU MATTER!

Take care of yourself in whatever way makes your soul happy.

If it's spending time in nature

Walk in the grass and let your feet feel the coolness of the earth underneath your body

Allow it to give you a comfort that connects you to it and yourself again

Feel the cool earth underneath you and embrace it's love and strength

Is it a good book?

Find a local bookstore, support a local author or read whatever your heart desires.

Get lost in a world that sets your soul on fire or your loins

♥

If it's a bath, and home spa day

Set the mood that will make it relaxing and rejuvenating to you and fulfill its purpose.

Just take care of YOU!

However you need to, self care is not only vital for a happy and healthy life, it's necessary

If we don't care for ourselves properly, who else will?

♥

## Never Settle

You deserve the absolute best life has to offer.

Never settle for crappy friends

Crappy jobs,

Crappy food,

Crappy homes

Crappy booze.

Always look for the best

Because YOU are the prize in the world

And deserve only platinum everything.

♥

# *Boxes*

People are comfortable

with others fitting in their idea of them into boxes.

Some are labeled as emotional,

hyper,

bitchy,

mean,

irritable,

sweet,

overbearing

or naive.

They put you in a box the moment they meet you

And rarely do you ever leave that specific box

of how they see you.

I say, burst through the metaphorical tape, and shred the box.

Be the you that you are, be damned.

Be the kind you.

♥

The bold you.

The mean you.

The strong you.

The powerful you.

The silent you.

The brave you.

Whatever you that is, you, be it.

Screw the boxes and be YOU!

♥

## *Gossip*

People will talk about you

when you are least expecting it.

They'll talk about you

when you are doing better than they are.

They'll talk about you

when you think they're your friend.

They talk because

they're insecure in themselves.

They talk because

they want what you have and can't accomplish it.

They are just mean.

There are a plethora of reasons,

but it doesn't really matter why they do it.

Just remember that those that do,

are not your people, they NEVER were!

♥

Be careful who you share your successes with.

Those that celebrate with you

may not always be there for YOU!

They may just want to stand in your sunlight

since they only  are capable of  darkness

♥

## *Endings*

Thank you, to all that have exited my life stage left.

You've taught me so much and I'm grateful,

Not just for the exit,

But for the lessons.

I stand taller and prouder now.

♥

## *Shine*

Be ok with shining

Be ok with not being liked

Be ok with not fitting in

Be ok with not being everyone's cup of tea

Be ok with being your own friend

There's so much comfort in knowing

that you don't have to please everyone.

That you don't have to get everyone to "like" you

and you don't have to care if they even do.

Find solace in knowing they don't,

cause they don't matter, YOU DO!

♥

## *Inner Strength*

Small, but mighty

Inner strength is far superior to outer

The inner confidence in our strength & abilities

Leaves us capable of handling any obstacle put in front of us.

No matter how small we may be

With inner strength we may as well be The Hulk ourselves, as we can tackle it all.

How you see yourself, defines your inner strength and abilities.

If you see yourself as broken or wounded, you will be.

But, if you see yourself as powerful & strong, you will be.

♥

## Soul

Go find your soul!

Do whatever lights your soul on fire and makes it dance!

Make yourself happy!

Make yourself feel brave!

Go find your soul,

embrace its warmth

and feel its bright glow reflecting.

# *Healing*

Take the time to heal your traumas

Take the space you need to grow from those traumas

Learn from them

Trauma is painful and damaging,

but it isn't something that can't be healed.

What you can't do is put a bandaid on it

And expect the massive hole of trauma

to be covered by a small bandaid.

Healing isn't linear and looks different for everyone

What works for one, won't work for another

Rip the bandaid off and begin the healing process

It's going to hurt

It's going to be long

But...It's going to be worth it!

♥

# It Won't Happen To Me

I said that about so many things…

And then life said, well, here you go.

Domestic violence, sexual abuse, mental abuse, sexual assault, betrayal, the list continues.

The point is simple, don't say, 'it will never happen to me'.

Because it can and will probably happen to you.

If it ever does, no matter what "it will never happen" is,

How you handle the aftermath is what makes you who you are.

My never's made me strong,

Decisively intent in my decisions on relationships and confident in my abilities.

It also gave me a higher appreciation for life and love than I had before.

At the end of the day, when someone goes through something horrible

If your first instinct is to say, "that will never happen to me"

Halt, think and know that it absolutely can.

♥

## *Love♥*

Oh that dreadful word

Love is the most desired feeling for some

Yet the most unattainable for others

Loving someone is beautiful, messy, difficult and work

You deserve the love that is the kind written in books and poetry

The kind that you consistently search for in others' relationships and admire

Don't settle until you find absolutely what you deserve

The person that will wholeheartedly love you, every bit, piece and morsel just as you are.

♥

## *Vent*

Be careful who you vent to...

Some just listen to share your troubles with others

Some just listen to belittle your fears

Some just listen to make themselves feel better

Some just listen to compare themselves to you

Some listen just to listen

But...

There are the rare gems that listen because they love you

Because they care and want to help you

Because they genuinely want to see you better yourself

Deciphering through those people is difficult

But once you do and you've chipped away at the fake ones

And found your diamonds in the rough; hold tight.

Those gems will get you through your darkest times and weakest moments.

They'll watch you soar and applaud your victories.

♥

They'll be your biggest cheerleaders and your warmest hugs when you are in need.

Be careful who you vent to.

♥

## *Magic*

It's like a light

It's like magic

It's like a beautiful butterfly

It's like the sound of rain

It's like the warmth of a hug

It's like a kiss from a loved one

Getting your insides right, makes everything feel intoxicating.

The world seems more beautiful.

Life seems more possible.

Problems seem less magnified because you now have the tools to tackle them.

Love yourself enough to know when you need help,

Seek it and then watch how your perspective on everything and everyone changes.

Some of those relationships you "thought" were so fantastic

You may find out were actually toxic to you and walking away is what is best for you.

Work on the inside and gloriously gaze as the outside shines.

♥

Let me be clear, your appearance is the least important thing about you.

But your ridiculously dope soul,

Your amazing thought process or your warm heart and kind nature,

Now, those are the things I gravitate towards.

♥

## *Be You*

Every word of this.

Be awkward.

Be funny.

Be intelligent.

Be kind.

Be weird.

Be quirky.

Be nerdy.

Be whatever you are.

Don't change YOU for anyone else!

♥

## *Narcissist*

The narcissistic mind is just a whirlwind playground.

They will make a problem and blame you.

Responsibility is never something

They would even think to take, for their actions.

Keep your eyes wide open for people like this,

Those victim players in scenarios of their own making,

They are the most dangerous.

♥

## *Trauma*

Trauma by definition is a deeply distressing or disturbing experience

-also, physical injury.

Trauma's come in all shapes and sizes.

All traumas don't look the same,

feel the same,

heal the same,

behave the same,

or even affect the individual the same.

Trauma in itself is a word that bears power.

But, so does healing.

Healing the trauma takes away its power

Trauma doesn't define who you are as a person,

It's just a fragment of who you are.

Your healing and what you do after that

IS what defines who you are.

Some think trauma broke them.

♥

I think mine gave me the courage to be who I was meant to be

And I don't look at that as broken anymore.

I look at my traumas as what I was able to survive through

And how much stronger it made me, not that it broke me.

Now, little things don't disturb me

Because I've been to war with abusers and won.

I wear those scars on me daily

Some visible, while others are internal

Neither are less painful or minimal

All are equivalent in their carnage.

♥

## *Storms*

Be the sun when they want thunder

Be the rainbow when they bring rain

Be the softness when they are the lightning

Be the light when they are dark

Be the warmth when they are cold

Shine brightly my friend, while others enjoy their clouds of sorrow

♥

## *Patience*

Pause

Breathe

Laugh

Enjoy the world around you

The colors

The smells

Be patient

Love

And then love again, harder.

Everything's coming together, in time.

You are just getting prepared for the glorious wonder that's coming.

♥

## *Peace*

Your peace is always more important

Than someone else's expectations of your reaction.

Silence,

Walking away and saying nothing at all

Gives you more peace than arguing or fighting to try and prove yourself or your point.

♥

## Compassion

Subtle, but effective differences.

Check your approach with others and see how you are treating them.

Strive for compassion in all you do.

It could change someone's life.

Sympathy and empathy are always amazing qualities to encompass, but pure and genuine

Compassion for another human is far superior.

♥

We are all bad in someone's story

No one is actually honest about the role they play in the demise of a relationship.

No one is actually honest even with themselves about their role they played in that demise

Unless they are truly self aware.

So, yes, we are all bad in someone else's story; and that's ok.

Why, you ask?

Because we know our truth.

We know what feelings and emotions led us to that ending and that decision to leave.

We know how the other person or people made us feel

And chose that we didn't like how it made us feel.

We choose ourselves and that is always OK!

Being the villain in someone else's story

Just means you were strong enough to not tolerate less than you deserve.

It means that you know your worth and for some it took a LONG time to figure that out.

♥

So wear that badge proudly,

Hold your head high and know that in choosing yourself,

You will be the bad one in someone else's story.

♥

## *Stay Strong*

Strong has always been my only option

Life hasn't gifted me with the golden road or the easy one.

So, I became strong instead, to deal with all that was thrown at me.

It made me catch it, readjust and throw it hard, away.

Call me the QB1 of strong.

Call me what you want, but I never give up.

Keep smiling and keep laughing always.

Even when I feel defeated inside.

♥

## *Action*

People always want to say things that sound like sugar coated deliciousness.

But at the end of the day, are they actually showing you the sweetest delight?

——Most likely, no.

When you ask them where this sugar coated yumminess went

And they can't give you a response or turn it around

And tell you why YOU are holding them back

from giving it to you; that is gaslighting.

So many relationships begin and end with manipulation and gaslighting.

Friendships, family and romantic relationships all fall victim to this.

Start to listen to your intuition.

If the yummy starts to not taste so sweet,

And the actions don't match up with the words, speak up.

If the person chooses not to alter their behavior

♥

Or they choose to gaslight you,

Walk away quickly or this will become your future.

Yes, love is wonderful and romantic

And everything that we as humans crave.

But what we crave more is being treated well,

Being authentically loved and respected

By a partner whose sole purpose is

To honor and protect us and our relationship,

Not manipulate it.

## *Flawed*

Top tier

Top shelf

Flawed...

It's all in how we look at ourselves.

Perspective

Our mistakes, our traumas, our hurt are just fragments of
what make us flawed and who we are;

They don't define, US.

Change how you look at yourself

And the world will follow...

♥

Don't look twice or adjust your eyes.

Believe them the first time, always.

People will always show you who they are and their true colors if you pay attention.

Don't look for what you WANT to see.

Look for what is actually there.

Look for what their actions actually show you.

In that, you find the truth.

♥

Stand for what's right...

Even if others sit.

Make your life beautiful...

Even if others think it's ugly.

Make your life meaningful...

Even if others don't understand.

Live for what you feel is right for YOU.

Fight for what YOU believe in.

Work towards goals that make YOU feel alive.

The opinions and beliefs of others are irrelevant

When it is comparable to yours.

Your life is yours to live and you only get one.

What you chose to do with it

And how you choose to live it is your choice.

Others can have opinions,

But the ultimate final decision is yours.

Have the courage to stand alone in a sea of imposters

♥

And those that don't think for themselves.

Have the eyes to see through the murky lies the world suffocates us with.

Have the strength to fight against the things

And the people whose sole purpose is to destroy others and inflict pain.

♥

## *Appreciation*

If you appreciate someone, tell them.

If you can't find the words, show them.

This simple act can change someone's life, day and outcome.

Let's inflict positive change on the world.

Negativity breeds negativity.

Positivity fuels positivity.

Let's collectively suffocate the negative

And breathe life into the positive and show appreciation for others.

♥

## *Smile*

Never forget how beautiful you are

Never let anyone tell you different

Never let anyone make you feel any less

You are beautiful

You are smart

You are amazing

You are incredible

You are remarkable

You are unique, You are kind

You are confident

You are the only you

Be you! Everyone else is taken

*Smile*

♥

You. Aren't. Your. Mistakes.

Sit with that.

Breathe it in.

Let it resonate.

Let it marinate.

Then remind yourself that everyone makes mistakes.

Mistakes don't define you, they change you.

Mistakes show your willingness to try.

You may not get it right the first time,

Hence the "mistake",

But assess and learn and don't repeat.

You. Are. Not. Your. Mistakes.

♥

You can cry

You can fall

You can throw things

You can feel defeated (for a moment)

You can be angry

You can be disappointed

You can feel disdain

But...

Get. Up!

Don't. Give. Up!

Brush it off, and keep going.

You allot yourself a few moments to feel the hurt,

Feel the loss, the disappointment

And then you RISE

like a Phoenix and become who you are supposed to be.

Strong people become strong not because they chose to,

But because they have to.

♥

# Selfies

Take those selfies for you ladies.

Fuck the rest of the world.

Drown them out.

Their opinions.

Their views.

Their lack of seeing your power.

Do your hair, or don't.

Put on makeup, or don't.

But take that selfie when you are feeling sexy, and even when you aren't.

Take it when you feel defeated.

Take it when you feel hurt.

Take it when you feel less than.

Take it to remind yourself what a badass, beautiful babe you are!

♥

No, I will not play your toxic game of Life.

I will however,

choose me,

in every way,

In every day and situation over you.

In case no one told you today....

You are exactly enough!

You are never TOO much!

You are beautiful inside & out!

You exude confidence and happiness!

Mistakes, they're proof you tried.

♥

## *Misery*

Misery is not more valuable than your happiness

No matter how much you may love someone,

Anyone.

♥

Aspire to be stunning for your mind

Gorgeous for your kindness

Breathtaking for your heart

And beautiful for your happiness

Not just simple labels like

Hot & sexy

♥

I forgive you for not speaking up

when you were being hurt.

I forgive you for staying

when the image you saw in the mirror

Was covered in bruises and blood.

I forgive you for thinking

those guys actually liked you

And you had a choice that night.

I forgive you for everything

you blocked out and then brought to light.

I forgive you for the anger

you held onto so deeply and intently.

I forgive you for hating your body

Because it was used as a playground for others.

I forgive you for every cut you put on you

To numb the inner pain that was unspoken.

I forgive you for convincing yourself

♥

Your children didn't deserve you as a mother.

I forgive you for trying to take your own life.

I forgive you.

♥

Never let anyone try and simmer your fire

Never let anyone try and dull your shine

Never let anyone try and steal your gifts

You are priceless

You are remarkable

You are relentless

You are magnetic

Be all feisty and shit!

Be the Queen of your own life

Grow your courage

Embrace your insecurities

Love your flaws

Laugh at your awkwardness

Fall in love with losing control of what comes next

♥

You've Changed

Thank you for noticing....

Thank you for seeing my growth...

For admiring my new feathers as I've shed the old wilted ones....

For noticing that I stand taller

Like a mighty oak and no longer like a puny pine...

For respecting my boundaries and needs in this new me...

And for giving me the grace that I needed to find her...

♥

Love doesn't hit

Love doesn't belittle

Love doesn't demean

Love doesn't disassemble

Love doesn't destroy

Love isn't supposed to hurt

Love is supposed to uplift

Love is supposed to wrap you up in its healing arms

And encourage you to be your highest self

♥

Dear little me,

You can begin to heal

You can let go of all that you endured

You were dealt cards that were painful

You've begun to grow

You've begun to scratch the surface

You've begun to hug little you

So...

Set the load down, whenever you're ready...

I'll be here ready to hold you and heal you when you are ready.

Signed,

Adult Me.

♥

Much like the rain washes away

The mistakes of the day,

Time lets the things that hurt us wash away.

♥

Life is all about perspective

If we look only at how someone let us down

We miss out on how someone showed us the lesson

We learned from that let down.

If we look only at how we feel about something

We miss out on seeing someone else's point of view

On the same subject

And giving us the ability to grow as a person

If we only listen to respond and not hear

We miss out on so much more

That people actually have to say

If we only enter relationships

Expecting to receive love but not give it back

We miss out on what an amazing gift love truly is

And to be loved genuinely and without conditions is

If we don't make those that love us feel safe

We make them fear us and in that fear,

♥

We have created a place where they

Are constantly questioning themselves

Is that love?

Is that what we deem fair?

Is that what you want for yourself?

♥

Embrace your flaws

And flaws in general

Imperfections make for a beautiful canvas

We all have them

We all avoid them like the plague

Instead of looking past them, let's embrace them.

Let's wear them like a warm sweater

And slide into them like a cozy pair of sweats.

It's the imperfections in us that make us who we are

And what draws others to us.

Those same imperfections

Are what make others like, and love us.

They see the beauty in our flaws,

Why can't we?

So, let's start!

Embrace your flaws.

Love your imperfections.

♥

The rest of us already do,

We've just been waiting on you.

♥

I reach for the phone to call you

Will you answer my call

Or will I just hear a generic voicemail

Instead of your buttery voice I crave?

Will you continue avoiding me,

Or will this be the time

The time you answer

The time you tell me why

Why you left me

With no explanation

Just gone...

I put the phone back down, another day I think.

I miss you

But is it really YOU I miss

Or the candy coated idea of you I created in my mind

The yummy you

The sweet you

♥

The tasty you

That I wanted to devour and savor all at the same time

Yeah...I miss you.

♥

I don't want to move on

I don't want to go on without you

I don't want to walk this life without you by my side

You want to move on

You want to do life without me

You want to dance through the night without me on your arm

Where do we meet in the middle?

The push and pull

The delicate distanced dance we are doing is tearing us apart

I just want us to be one again

You look at me

Sternly he demands we be apart

I have no choice

He has made the decision for us both

I am powerless

♥

I thought of you today

But that is no different than yesterday

I smelled your side of the bed

Where you last laid your head

You scent

That intoxicating decadent aroma

Is now gone

I walked by the lake

Where we used to walk hand in hand

It looks different now

It's not full of beauty and life anymore

It's somber and dark

I thought of you today

But, then again

I think of you every day

All day...

♥

She walks with a confidence that seems like she is dancing

But I hear no music

Head held high, clothes perfectly pressed like a movie star

But I am not watching a movie

She casually flips her hair in the wind

And smiles softly while strutting along

But why am I enchanted now?

She moves like she is floating on air

With delicate steps that contain purpose and poise

I am intoxicated

She is coming towards me and warmly smiling,

Her eyes crinkle and her face softens

I am sweating and nervous

She speaks, so eloquently and intelligent

I am mesmerized

I have realized that I want to be like her.

I want to walk with ease into a room and command people to notice me

♥

Without doing anything but being there and being me,
confidently so

I want to be her

♥

I call and call

But you never answer

Why?

You left me, why would you do that to me?

You said you would never leave me

You said you would be there forever

Is your definition of forever different from mine?

Or was I just not your forever?

I long for your voice

Your breath on my neck

Your touch on my skin

To smell you again on my clothes

But you stole that from me

You stole forever

Thief.

♥

Magic...

You may have to squint

You may have to close your eyes

You may have to look quickly

But...

If you pay attention

It's there, subtly

There is magic in every day

In every moment

In every person you meet

Look for it and once you find it

Embrace it and nurture it

So the rest of the world can find it too

♥

Clawing, scratching, dragging me away

I am burning with fear

The sound of the thumping and banging is becoming almost melodic

The cool red that flows down my face and arms is somehow soothing me

It's crimson stream is clouding my vision and I begin to feel sleepy

There is that damn thumping again

Oh the pain in my head, my whole body aches now

My eyes feel so very heavy

I can't breathe

I can't speak

I can't see

Bright white light surrounds me

I feel it's warmth and I embrace it like a cashmere sweater

The crimson sea around me fades

The pain in my body lessens until it is nonexistent

I exhale one hard long breath

♥

I look down and see the crimson and purple covering me

I see that thumping and dragging

But I have won, I am now gone

Finally safe and home.

♥

Out the window I look

At days passing by

At strangers laughing and walking carefree

At the world moving along at it's own pace

While I sit drowning

Barely holding my head above water

Out the window I look

At nights gone by

At lovers walking hand in hand

Kissing sweet soft delicious love into each other

Fighting and then making up so quickly

While I sit drowning in my own sorrow

My own broken heart

Oh how I long to be one of those strangers

Living for each moment

For each kiss, each hand held, each laugh

But, I sit, starring

♥

Drowning.

♥

You were delicately mine

I savored every moment we shared

I treasured the poetic touches of your hands on my body

Of your kiss on my lips, I long for those lips

Oh how they tasted like love, and then quickly betrayal

Our love was chaotic and beautiful

Cursive writing it's way through my heart

You, that smile, that touch; I hate you

I hate that you made me love you

I hate that you made me envision a perfect love with you

I hate that you stole our future with your selfish act

I hate that you turned

Our beautiful cursive into serial killer writing.

You murdered our love.

I'm hopeless

I'm jealous

I'm envious

I'm flawed

I'm human

But...

I'm hopeful

I'm strong

I'm enlightened

I'm imperfect

I'm loved

I'm me

And the only one like me

Take it or leave it.

♥

Your approval was never needed

You thought it was

But it never was

I never needed you to like me

I never cared if you did

I never needed you to stand behind my decisions

They were mine to make and the consequences were mine to endure

But you insisted upon inserting yourself regardless

So, where did that get you?

On the outside looking in, didn't it.

How's the view?

♥

I run my hands across my body

Feeling its curves and dimples

Those same ones that I looked at before and shied away from

Now, I see them and smile

Now, I see them and blush

How could I have hated them?

How could I have been so cold to my own skin?

I am perfectly made rings in my ears

Love myself I repeat over and over

I look into the mirror and stare at my naked skin and embrace it

It's beautiful

It's round in some places and curvy in others

But, it's all beautiful because it is me.

♥

I love me

I love who I am

I love who I am becoming

I love who I was

I love who I wasn't

I love who I tried to be

I love who I thought I was

I love what I have done

I love what I will do

I hate what I have done to some

I hate what others have to do me

But, I love me, finally and wholeheartedly.

You returned again

Like a plague

Like a predictable hurricane season

Like a dog needing to eat

Like herpes

You always come back

Just fucking leave.

Leave me
ALONE ♥

♥

The lines on my face could tell so many stories

They could tell you of the time the cat ran across my face and tore it open

Or the time the dog ripped my face open

Or when my brother dropped a toy on my forehead

Or when he split my lip open

Or when he broke my nose

Those lines by my eyes

Those come from my children

From laughing with them

From loving them

From them loving me and watching them live

The ones around my mouth,

Those come from smiling at my friends, and children

Of happy days and hopeful moments

The ones between my eyes,

Those come from fear

Fear that he will find me again and this time

♥

This time, he will kill me

So instead, I focus on those line on my eyes and mouth

The ones that remind me of happiness and not fear

Of love and life not death.

♥

*Embrace your flaws and flaws in general.*
*Imperfections make for a beautiful canvas.*

*-k.m. brady*

*It's not about the feeling of the intensity, it's about*
*the joy in the consistency.*

*-k.m. brady*

Thank you for peaking into my poetic thoughts.
I'll catch you in the next book.

♥

♥

Made in the USA
Middletown, DE
24 August 2022

71624371R00083